It's a FROG'S Life

Kath Murdoch and **Stephen Ray**

Dedicated to our godson Sam Turner.
Special thanks to Garry Werren and Gerry Marantelli.

Written by Kath Murdoch and Stephen Ray
Illustrated by Ian Forss
Designed by Christine Deering
Picture research by Brigitte Zinsinger

Published by Mimosa Publications Pty Ltd
PO Box 779, Hawthorn 3122, Australia
© 1995 All rights reserved

Literacy 2000 is a Trademark registered in the
United States Patent and Trademark Office.

Distributed in the United States of America by

Rigby

A Division of Reed Elsevier Inc.
500 Coventry Lane
Crystal Lake, IL 60014
800-822-8661

Distributed in Canada by
PRENTICE HALL GINN
1870 Birchmount Road
Scarborough
Ontario M1P 2J7

99
10 9 8 7 6 5
Printed in Hong Kong through Bookbuilders Ltd

ISBN 0 7327 1568 7

Contents

Frog Country

Have you ever been walking near a pond or a swamp and heard croaking sounds coming from the water? If you'd followed the sounds and looked very closely, you might have caught sight of one of the creatures – but, then again, you might not . . .

Seeing frogs is not always easy; they usually hide themselves in mud, between rocks, in grass, or even in trees so that they won't become dinner for hungry predators.

Frogs and Toads

There are more than 3,000 species of frogs. Each species has its own particular characteristics, but most frogs are soft and moist, with bulging eyes, wide mouths, and strong back legs. Toads usually have drier, sometimes "warty" skin, and fatter bodies.

Frogs and toads together make up one *group* of the scientific family known as *amphibians*. "Frogs" is the overall common name for this group.

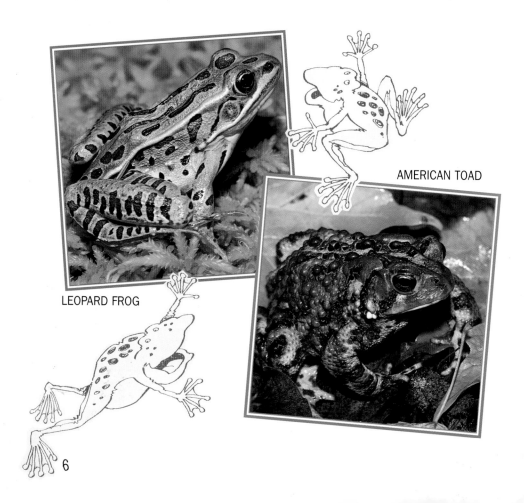

AMERICAN TOAD

LEOPARD FROG

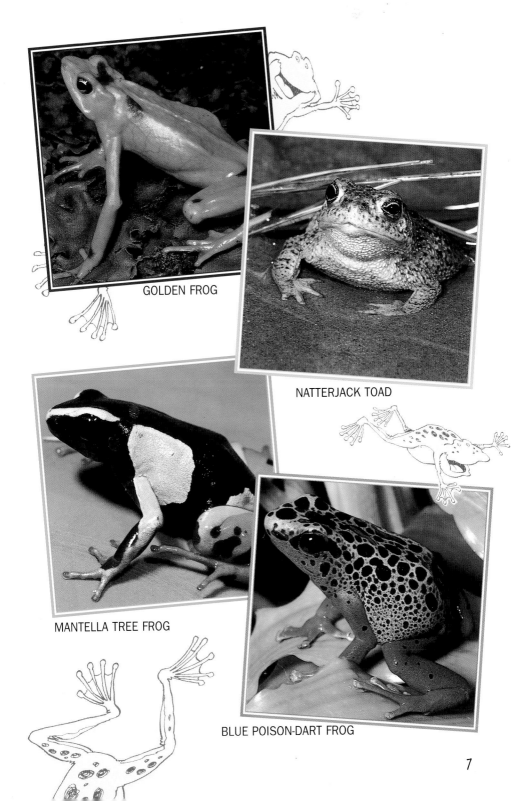

GOLDEN FROG

NATTERJACK TOAD

MANTELLA TREE FROG

BLUE POISON-DART FROG

7

Habitats

There are frogs and toads living in many different environments, in almost every country in the world.

COMMON TOAD

Some species spend most of their lives on the ground, in swamps, or around lakes, ponds, and streams. Others live in trees in warm, damp rain forests; and some species survive in hot, dry, desert environments.

RED-EYED TREE FROG

Although frogs and toads can be found far and wide throughout the world, all their habitats have one important "ingredient" in common – fresh water.

Australian water-holding frogs live in the desert. They spend most of their lives under the ground, out of the drying sun. They enclose themselves in waterproof sacs to hold in their precious moisture.

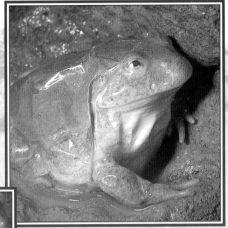

When it does rain, the frogs break out of their sacs to absorb as much water as they can.

Fascinating Frog Fact

In desert areas, Australian Aborigines sometimes used water-holding frogs to provide water to drink.

The frogs swell with water, which they use to survive until the next rainfall; this might be years away.

Froggy Features

Frogs and toads have short front legs and longer, strong back legs. They don't have necks, tails, fur, or scales; their bodies are soft and rounded.

Many frogs and toads have big bulging eyes on the top of their heads – this enables them to have a clear view while their bodies are concealed in mud or under water.

BROWN STRIPED FROG

Fascinating Frog Fact

Some frogs can stay under water for hours! This is because oxygen in the water can pass through their thin skin.

All frogs and toads are *cold-blooded*; their bodies don't stay at a constant temperature, but change according to their surroundings.

Although they have some important features in common, each species is different. Frogs and toads have just the right features for survival in their environment. Some species are big and others are tiny; some have padded feet and others have pointed toes. And although some frogs are green, frogs can be many different colors.

HARLEQUIN FROG

The red-eyed frog from Australia has sticky pads on its toes which enable it to move around in trees without falling.

Leap, Crawl, Climb

Most frogs and toads can jump, but they get around in lots of other ways, too. Some creep along the ground. Others climb through trees. And some remarkable frogs even glide from one tree to another, using their big webbed feet like parachutes.

Fascinating Frog Fact

At a frog jumping competition, a South African sharp-nosed frog covered more than 4.5 meters in a single jump. This is like a person jumping over the length of 6 buses.

COMMON TOADS

LEOPARD FROG

WALLACE'S FLYING FROG

SPOTTED GRASS FROG

Whether they are are leapers, creepers, or gliders, most frogs and toads are superb swimmers. Their strong back legs and streamlined shapes help them move swiftly through the water.

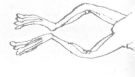

Predators

Frogs can become meals for other animals. Many birds and snakes eat frogs, and much of a frog's life is spent trying to avoid the strong beaks and jaws of these predators.

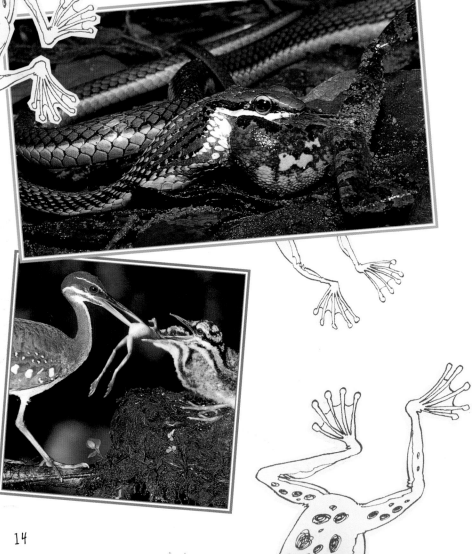

Camouflaged against the leaves in its habitat, the Malaysian horned frog can often escape danger by staying still.

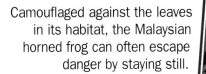

Some toads make themselves look bigger to try to scare enemies away.

Many poisonous frogs, like this poison-arrow frog, are brightly colored. Predators learn to recognize them – and to avoid them.

Fascinating Frog Fact

As little as 0.0001 gram of poison from the skin of the Koikoi arrow frog from South America could kill a person.

15

Food for Frogs

Frogs and toads have varied diets. Insects, snails, grubs, worms, and spiders can be food for frogs and toads. So can mice, bats, and even other frogs.

Fascinating Frog Fact

Frogs help to control many insect pests. The common toad eats more than 10,000 insects each summer.

Most frogs have a sticky tongue which can be flicked out at lightning speed to catch unsuspecting prey.

The Surinam toad has no tongue. It feeds on dead creatures at the bottom of lakes, so it doesn't need a lightning-fast tongue.

But no matter what they eat, frogs gulp their food down whole. They use their teeth to grip their prey – not to chew it.

HORNED
FROG

GREEN
TREE FROG

Fascinating Frog Fact

Many frogs blink as they swallow. This pushes the eyes back into the head and helps to push the food down the throat.

COMMON TOAD

Croaking

Different species of frogs make different croaking noises. But it is only the males of the species that croak. They make the sound by pushing air across their vocal cords, making them vibrate. The sound is amplified by loose skin, known as the vocal sac, which puffs out as the sound is made.

Croaking helps frogs and toads to identify one another and to mark out their territories. It is also important in finding a mate.

Some species have a single vocal sac under the throat. Others have a vocal sac on each side of the throat.

Laying and Looking After Eggs

In the mating season, the calls of male frogs and toads attract females of the same species.
In most species, a male frog clasps a female with his front legs until she releases eggs, and then he releases sperm to fertilize them. The fertilized eggs are called *frog spawn.*

The clasping of a female frog by a male frog is called *amplexus.*

Gray tree frogs lay their eggs in groups in trees.
They beat the spawn into a foamy nest with their back legs.

Most species of frogs lay their eggs in water and then leave their spawn unguarded. But some species have remarkable ways of protecting their young.

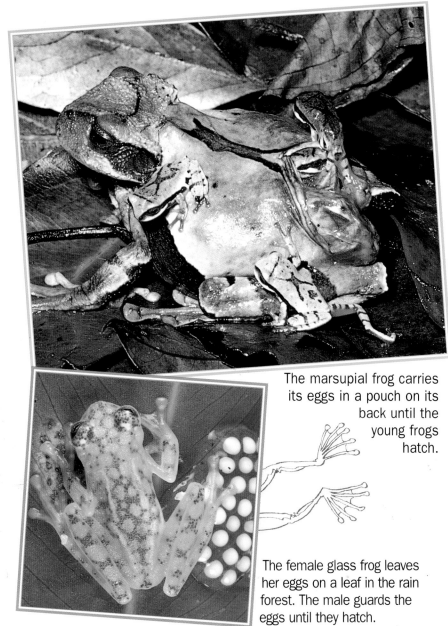

The marsupial frog carries its eggs in a pouch on its back until the young frogs hatch.

The female glass frog leaves her eggs on a leaf in the rain forest. The male guards the eggs until they hatch.

The poison-dart frog carries its tadpoles on its back.

Gray tree frogs are kept safe in their frothy nest in the trees. When the tadpoles hatch, they drop into the water below.

The male midwife toad carries the eggs on his back until the tadpoles hatch.

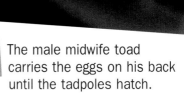

Tadpoles

Inside each egg is a black speck, which, if conditions are right, will eventually become a frog.

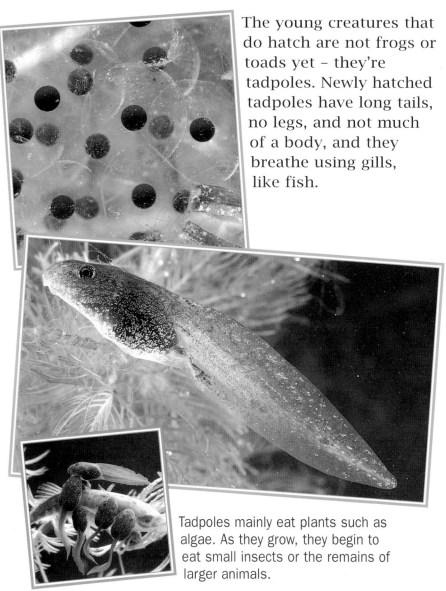

The young creatures that do hatch are not frogs or toads yet – they're tadpoles. Newly hatched tadpoles have long tails, no legs, and not much of a body, and they breathe using gills, like fish.

Tadpoles mainly eat plants such as algae. As they grow, they begin to eat small insects or the remains of larger animals.

But they don't stay like this for long. They go through a complete change, known as *metamorphosis.*

Tadpoles wriggle around in the water,
eating as much as they can. Their back legs soon begin to grow. Then, as the tadpoles develop lungs, they use their new legs to swim to the surface to breathe.

Next the front legs grow and the tadpoles' bodies become more frog-shaped.

Last of all, the tail disappears, and the young frog is ready to leave the water.

Fascinating Frog Fact

Different kinds of frogs take different amounts of time to develop – from three weeks to three years.

Fascinating Frog Fact

Some species, such as the rain frog from Costa Rica, change from tadpoles to tiny frogs before they hatch.

Natural Danger

Danger is a natural part of frogs' lives. Of all the eggs each female lays, only a few become fully developed frogs. The rest are eaten by birds, fish, snakes, and sometimes even other frogs. Some eggs never hatch because the conditions are not quite right for tadpoles to grow.

Adult frogs face many perils, too. As well as being alert to the constant danger of lurking predators, frogs must not let their moist skin dry out.

By spending a lot of time in water, frogs can avoid the drying sun.

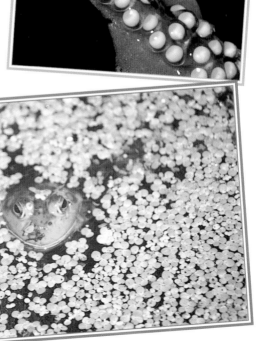

New Dangers

Many species of frogs are in danger of becoming extinct. Many frog habitats are being changed or destroyed by people. Without a food supply, shelter, and the conditions they need to breed, frogs cannot survive.

Already, some species of frogs are extinct. Others haven't been seen for many years and may be gone forever.

Most scientists believe that frogs are especially sensitive to changes in the environment, such as pollution of waterways and the thinning of the ozone layer.

The gastric brooding frog hasn't been seen in the wild for the last ten years.

All around the world, people are working to protect frogs and their habitats. Everyone can help by looking after the environment and trying not to cause pollution.

Some zoos breed endangered species and release them into the wild. Frogs in captivity are monitored closely to ensure that the artificial environment provides the right conditions for survival.

Scientists who study frogs, other amphibians, and reptiles are called *herpetologists*.

Out of Balance

When frogs and toads live in their natural habitats, they are part of a balanced ecosystem. Moving them into a new habitat can disrupt the natural balance of that environment, and this can have disastrous effects.

Fascinating Frog Fact

The female cane toad can lay as many as 60,000 eggs in a year.

About 60 years ago, people introduced a species of South American toad into areas of Australia to help control a beetle that was destroying the sugarcane crops. These toads, which became known as cane toads, had no natural predators in Australia. They adapted well to their new home, and their numbers grew rapidly.

Today, cane toads exist in plague proportions in many areas of Australia, eating many kinds of natural wildlife, but not the beetle they were brought in to eat. Cane toads are threatening the environment in another way, too. Their skin contains a deadly poison which quickly kills most animals that try to eat them.

The Amphibian Family

All frogs and toads are amphibians. Amphibians are one of the five families of animals with backbones. Amphibians have several features in common: they spend part of their lives in water and part on land, they are cold-blooded, and they have moist skin.

Frogs and toads make up one group of amphibians; salamanders, newts, and caecilians make up the other three groups.

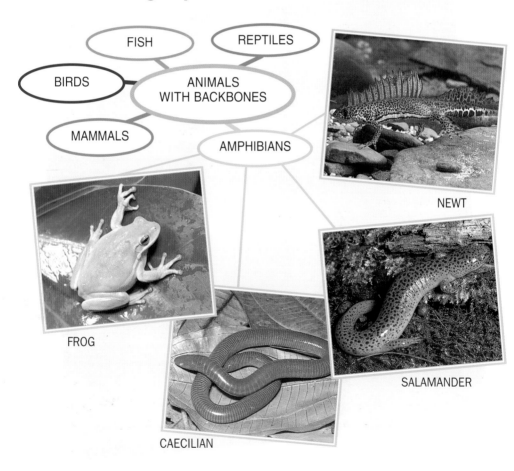

FISH

REPTILES

BIRDS

ANIMALS
WITH BACKBONES

MAMMALS

AMPHIBIANS

NEWT

FROG

SALAMANDER

CAECILIAN

Glossary

amplexus –
the clasping of a female frog by a male as she releases her eggs

frog –
the common name for one of the four groups of amphibians

spawn –
fertilized frog eggs

herpetologists –
scientists who study amphibians and reptiles

metamorphosis –
a complete change from one thing into another. Tadpoles undergo a metamorphosis to become frogs.

toad –
common name for many frog-like amphibians

ozone layer –
layer of gas in the atmosphere which shields Earth from the sun's harmful energy rays

species –
a group of animals who have very similar characteristics

vocal sac –
loose skin under or at the sides of the throat which puffs out to amplify frogs' croaking sounds

Index

TITLES IN THE SERIES

Auscape International: *Kathie Atkinson* (brown striped frog, page 10); *Jean-Paul Ferrero* (cane toad, page 29); *C. A. Henley* (spotted grass frog, page 13); *D. Parer and E. Parer-Cook* (water-holding frog, page 9; green tree frog, page 17; gastric brooding frog, page 26). **Australian Picture Library:** *Peter Menzel* (polluted water, page 26); *Larry Mulvehill* (children at pond, page 4); *Zefa, Rauschenbach* (frog catching insect, page 16). **Michael Bentley:** (frog in duckweed, page 25). **Brian Rogers/Biofotos:** (red-eyed tree frog, page 8). **Bruce Coleman:** *Jane Burton* (Surinam toad, page 16; tadpoles eating, page 22); *Jeff Foott* (salamander, page 30); *M. P. L. Fogden* (golden frog, page 7; toad page 15; tree frogs, page 19, tree frog spawn, pages 21); *C. B. & D. W. Frith* (tree frog on tap, back cover); *Udo Hirsch* (newt, page 30); *Felix Labhardt* (common toads, page12; frogs in amplexus, page 19); *Andrew J. Purcell* (natterjack toad, page 7); *Marie Read* (American toad, page 6); *Hans Reinhard* (frog with double vocal sac, page 18; frog, page 30); *John Shaw* (leopard frog, page 6; frog with single vocal sac, page 18). **Michael and Patricia Fogden:** (blue poison-dart frog, page 7; red-eyed frog, page 11; birds and frog, page 14; marsupial frog, page 20; tadpole developing in egg, page 24; snake eating eggs, page 25). **Heather Angel:** (frog, contents page and page 24; poison-arrow frog page 15; Malaysian horned frog, page 15; midwife toad, page 21); **David Johns:** (herpetologist, page 27). **Oxford Scientific Films:** *G. I. Bernard* (toad eating mouse, page 17; tadpoles pages 22-24); *Stephen Dalton* (frog jumping, page 12); *Michael Fogden* (red-eyed leaf frog, cover; harlequin frog, page 11; poison-dart frog, page 21; caecilian, page 30). **The Photo Library - Sydney:** (glass frog, page 20). **Planet Earth Pictures:** *Andre Bartschi* (horned frog, page 5; frog eating insect, page 17); *J. R. Brackgirdle* (water and lilies, cover); *Philip Chapman* (Wallace's flying frog, page 13); *Carol Farneti* (snake eating frog, page 14); *Nick Garbutt* (mantella tree frog, page 7); *Steve Hopkin* (common frog, cover); *Chris Howes* (bullfrog, cover); *P. J. Palmer* (frog spawn, page 22); *Vincent Serventy* (water-holding frog, page 9). **Klaus Uhlenhut:** (cane toads, page 28).